THIS BOOK BELONGS TO

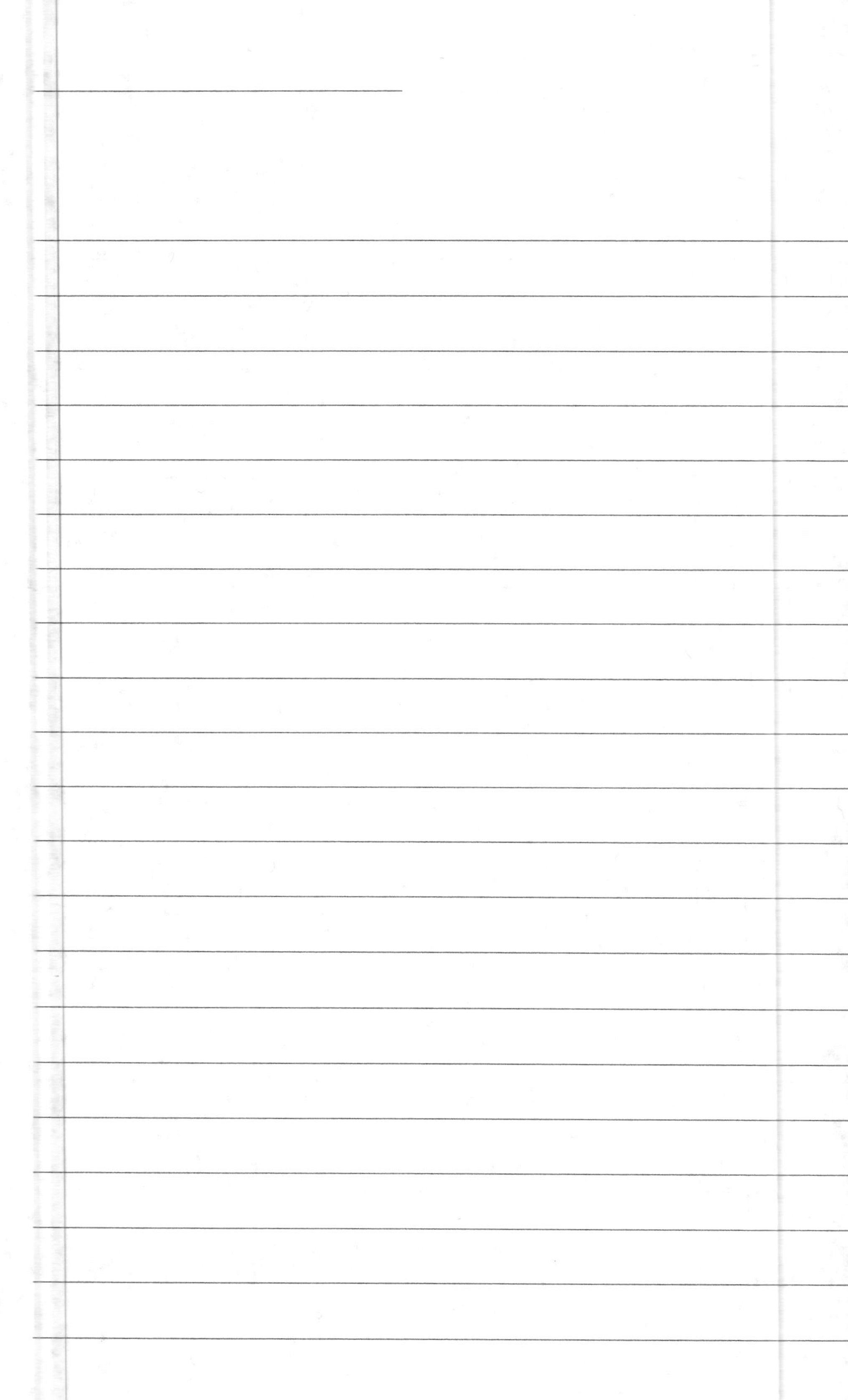

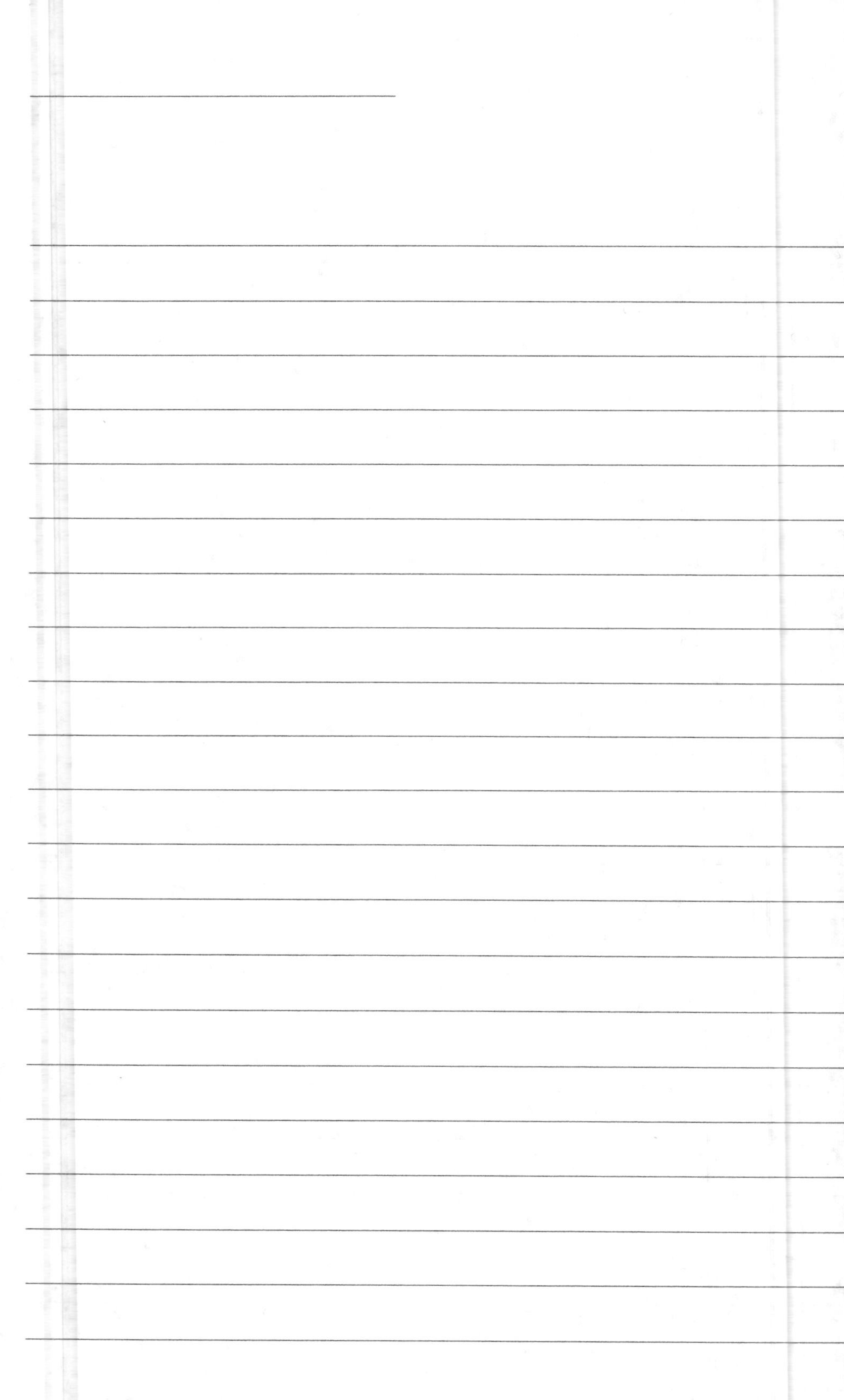

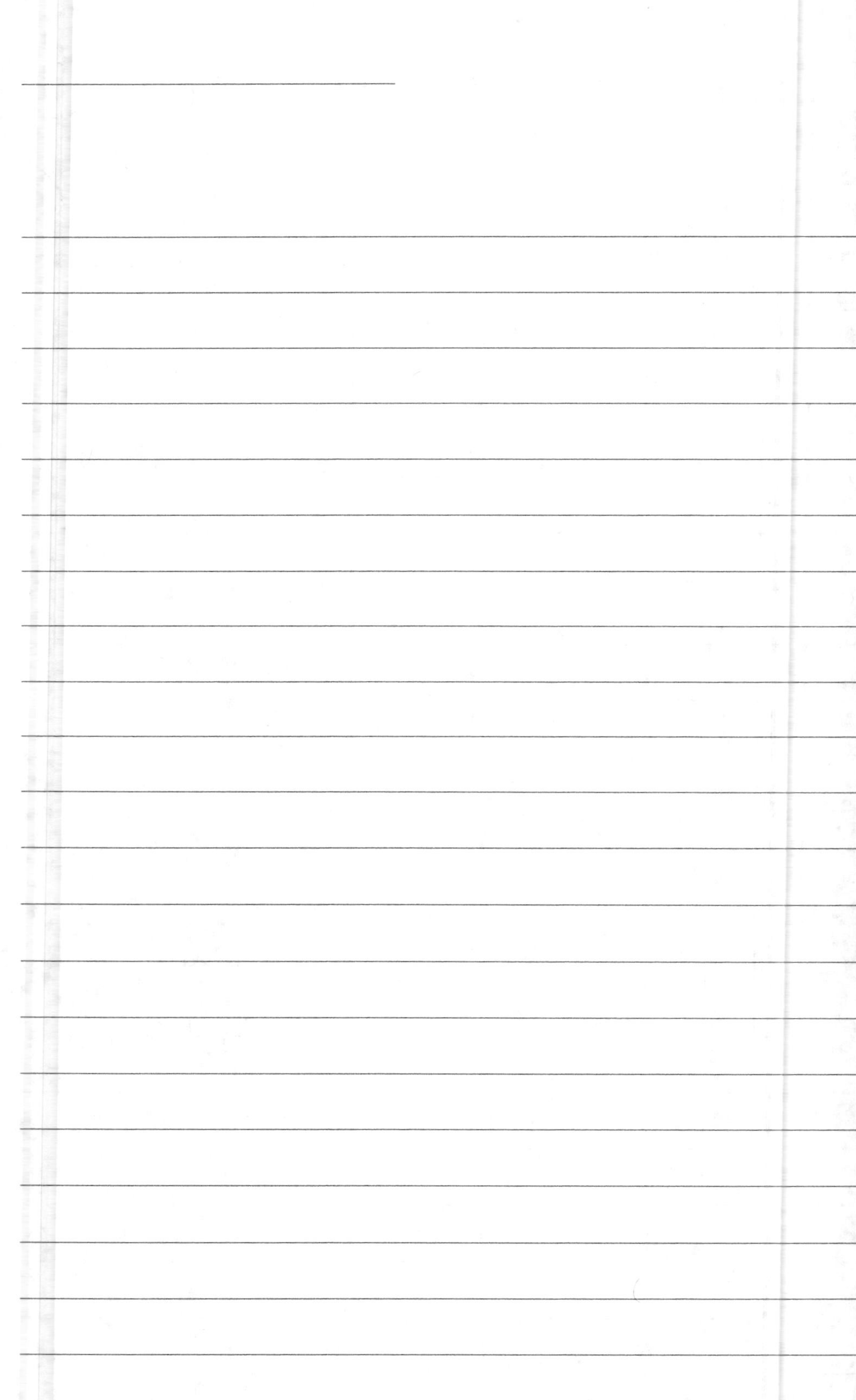

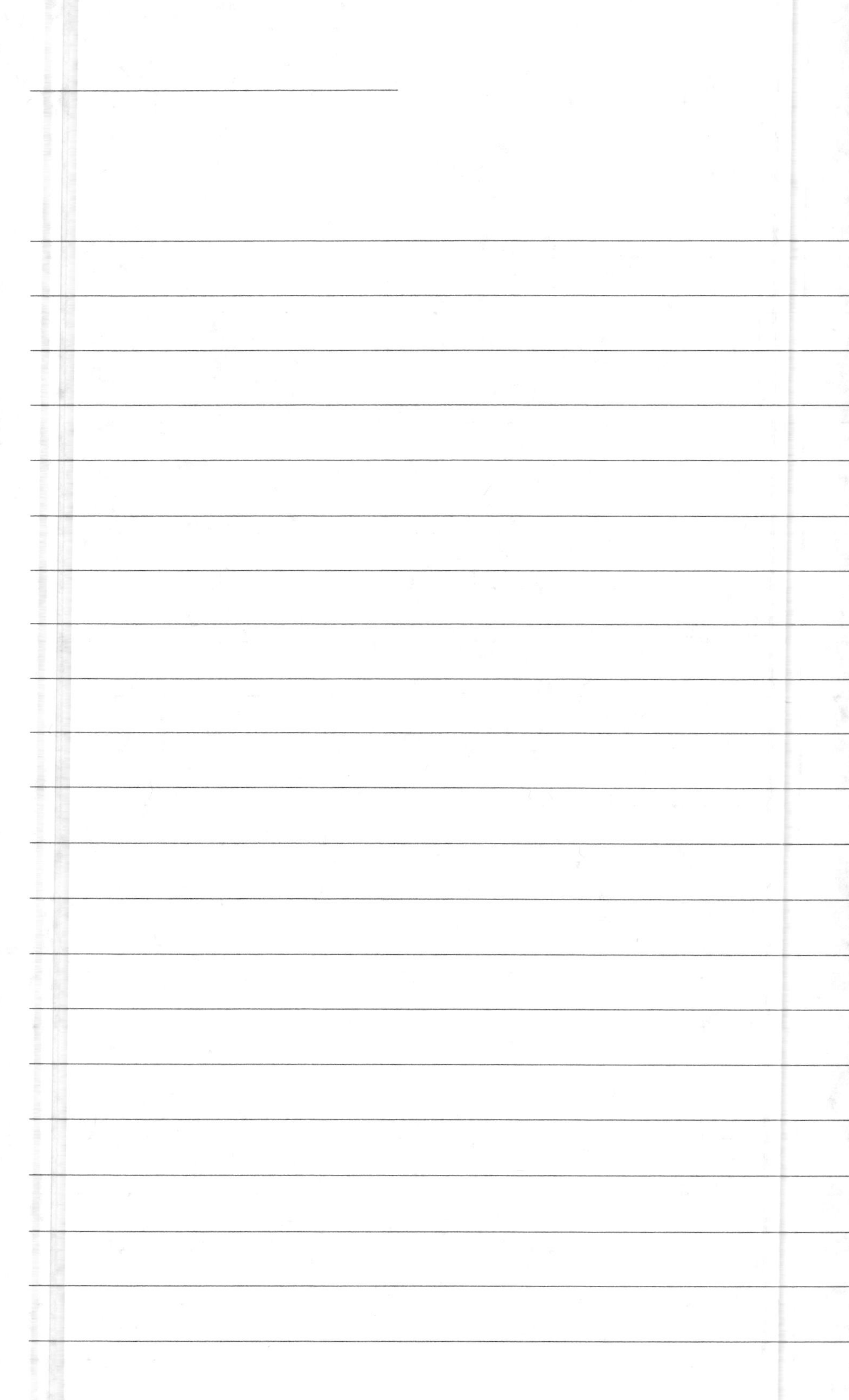

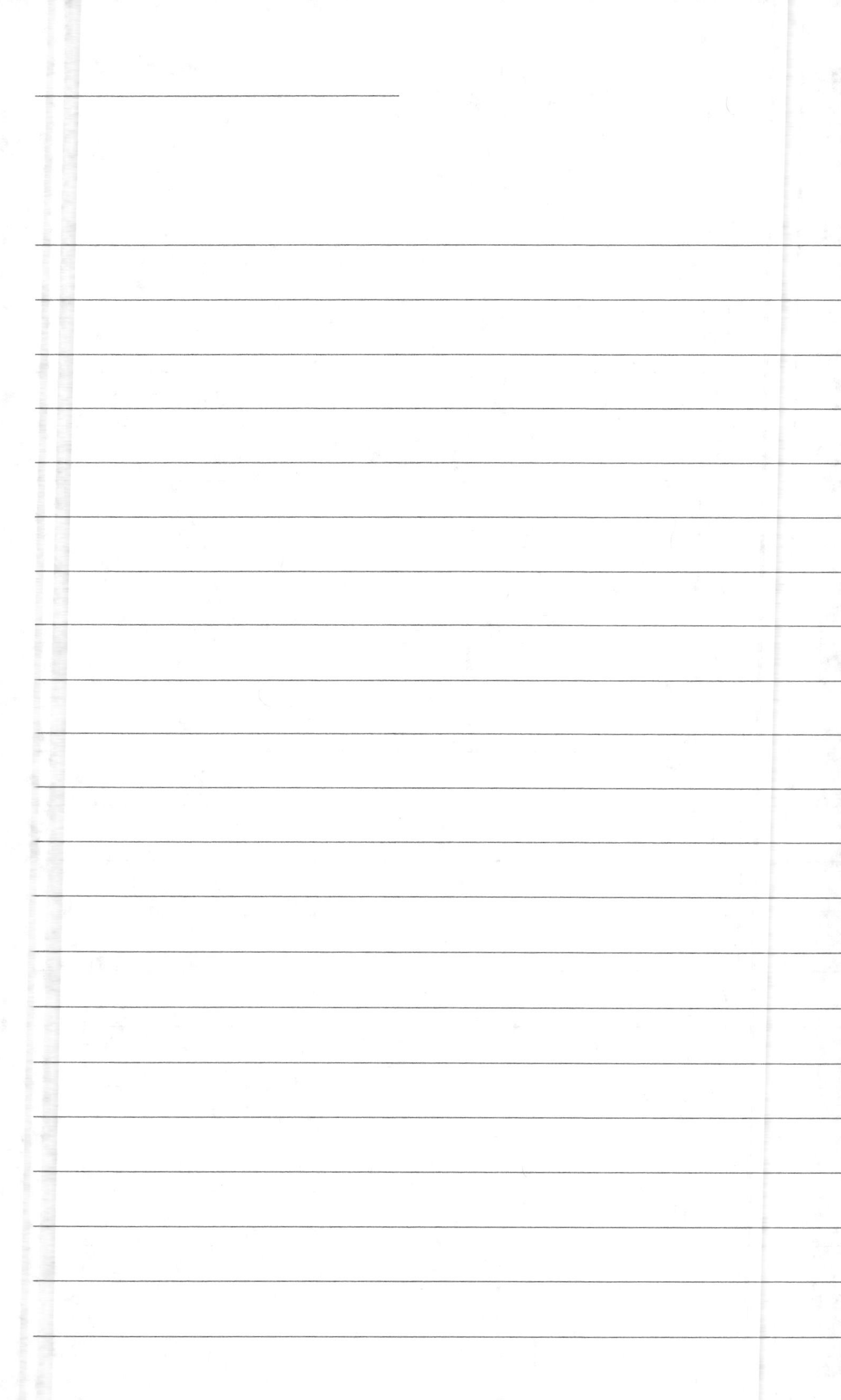